D0981569

the little book of

SITCOM

by John
Vorhaus

Bafflegab Books
a wholly-owned subsidiary of Nonrandom House
356 Hill Street
Monrovia, CA 91016

ISBN: 1477526226
ISBN-13: 978-1477526224

Also by John Vorhaus

The Comic Toolbox: How To Be Funny Even If You're Not

Creativity Rules! A Writer's Workbook

Killer Poker: Strategy and Tactics for Winning Poker Play

Killer Poker Online

The Killer Poker Hold'em Handbook

Poker Night

Killer Poker Online/2

Killer Poker No Limit

Decide to Play Great Poker (with Annie Duke)

Decide to Play Drunk Poker

Fiction

Under the Gun

The California Roll

The Albuquerque Turkey

World Series of Murder

Lucy in the Sky

to Ryan and Madison
because why the hell not?

the little book of

SITCOM

Here's the Good News

It took me six months to write my first sitcom script. The next one took three. I knocked off the third one in about six weeks, and I continued to get faster and faster as I learned more and more about everything from how to format a script to how to turn unfunny jokes into funny ones. Last week I wrote a sitcom script in four and a half hours. It was an ugly first draft – first drafts are ugly by definition – but I got from *fade in* to *fade out* in a single afternoon's work, and to me that's not nothing. So if you've embarked upon a sitcom writing career, and especially if it's early days for you, I want to give you some good news from somewhat further down the line: you'll get better and you'll get faster. You can kick this thing's ass.

It'll never be as easy as you'd like it to be. You'll never stop struggling to find the perfect turn of phrase or joke, or character key, or that one plot twist that resolves your story in a surprising, satisfying and rewarding way. You'll never entirely free yourself from those awful moments of staring out the window, wondering why your brain is broken or where your next good idea will come from. You'll always have moments where you think, "I suck," and no amount of pep-talkery from others (and no quantity of overproof rum) will persuade you otherwise. But those moments will pass. You will solve your story problems. You will have good ideas. You will write jokes that are funny the first time, the next time, every time. You will get better at your craft, and eventually you will master it. Why? A couple of reasons.

First, writing sitcoms isn't really that hard. So much of what you need to know is already defined for you. You know that your script needs to be a certain short length, with a certain small number of characters. You know that your choice of scenes is limited to your show's standing sets and maybe one or two swing sets or outside locations. You know how your characters behave and how they're funny, either because you invented them or because you're writing for a show where these things are already well established. Sitcom is easy and sitcom is fun. Sitcom is the gateway drug to longer forms of writing. It's a pretty good buzz and a pretty good ride, a great way to kill an afternoon, or even six months.

Second, improvement happens naturally. Every time you write a sitcom script you get a little better at it. You learn how to avoid dead-end stories. You learn how to enter a scene as late as possible and leave it as soon as possible. You learn how to avoid *chuffa,* the boring bullshit that slows down a story or scene, or as it's otherwise known, *tomando café* – drinking coffee – meaningless moments where people are just sitting around talking about nothing. You learn how to stay out of joke deserts, where pages and pages of dialogue roll by but nothing particularly hilarious happens.

And you learn all of this organically, almost subconsciously, simply by attacking over and over again the problems peculiar to writing a sitcom script. Now, are you ready for the great news? *This education takes place even if what you're writing is not particularly good.* It's true. No matter how badly you suck on the page, you're always learning something new about your craft, and thus steadily (okay, in fairness sometimes unsteadily) moving toward a time when you generally don't suck. All you have to do is keep writing. The learning takes care of itself.

That said, no one around you will tell you that mastering this craft is a snap. It takes a lot of work: hours and days and weeks and months of creative labor and skull sweat, trying to turn nothing into something. It's hard on the ego to face rejection and revision and notes and suggestions from yammerheads who may or may not know what they're talking about. It challenges your resolve when people around you (maybe your nearest and dearest) tell you that you're wasting your time. It takes a toll on your social life when writing your next script is more important than seeing friends, doing laundry, taking a shower. There's doubt, fear, procrastination, alienation, poverty, writer's block, writer's cramp and dozens of other real and imagined setbacks, hurdles, distractions and delays. It would be fully disingenuous to pretend that these roadblocks don't exist – yet that's exactly what I want you to do. There's a name for this strategy. It's called *adopting a useful fiction.*

A useful fiction is a certain sort of lie we tell for the sake of moving past barriers and moving closer to our goals. If you believe me when I tell you that writing sitcoms is easy, you'll be more motivated to try, because just generally we'd rather do things that are easy than are hard. If I tell you (or you tell yourself) that you'll get better at your craft, then you'll cast loose the air of hopelessness that might otherwise engulf you. You'll push ahead, having such writing days as you are able to until you find to your surprise and delight that you are, in fact, getting better at your craft. In this sense we can say that a useful fiction is a self-fulfilling prophecy. You might say that it's a case of "fake it till you make it," or of having faith in your ability at a time when evidence is absent. No matter how you look at it, a useful fiction is a fiction, but it's useful just the same.

So right now I'm asking you to adopt this specific useful fiction: *You can do it.* Go ahead and say it right out loud. Yes, it's dumb, but it's not the dumbest thing you'll do in your career, or even today. And even if you don't believe it, you have to agree that saying, "I can do it" is a whole lot more uplifting, more enabling, and more likely to breed success than saying, "I can't do it." That's the power of the useful fiction, and that's exactly how it works. You tell yourself you can do a thing for the sake of being able to do that thing, because you know for sure that if you tell yourself you can't, well, you won't.

I've been writing situation comedies for more than a quarter of a century, and showing others how to do it for nearly as long. I've taught and trained writers all over the world – 28 countries on four continents at last count. Along the way, by closely examining my writing process and the process of others, I've developed some pretty slick tricks, and it is these tricks that I intend to share with you here. Because it's not enough just to sell you the useful fiction that sitcom is easy. I want to *make* it easy. I want to help you find shortcuts, see creative problems clearly, and generate solutions you can trust. I want to help you be funny and I want to help you be sure-handed in story. You'll find some of these techniques to be immediately useful; others will not really bear fruit until you're somewhat further advanced in your craft. But they'll all help in the same way: by demystifying the creative process, and making it easier and more enjoyable for you to do what you do.

So let's have some fun, shall we? Because this is sitcom writing, after all. As jobs go, it's not a hard one. We get to work indoors, sitting on our rhumbas. We don't punch a clock. We play and invent and create. I remember once running a story meeting on an episode involving a woman's decision to get breast augmentation surgery. At the conclusion of the meeting I said, "Do you realize we just spent the entire afternoon talking about boob jobs?" Sitcom. It's nice work if you can get it. And you can get it if you try. That's the good news, and it's not even a lie.

Okay, let's start by slaying everyone's favorite dragon: writer's block. It'll be nice to have that out of the way.

How to Beat
Writer's Block Forever

Almost the minute I started writing, I started wasting time, on everything from emails and Xbox to Minesweeper and stupid fricking solitaire. I'm not alone in this. All writers waste time. Sometimes we do it because we're not quite ready or able to solve the story or script problem at hand, and we need more time to let our thoughts marinate. Often, though, we squander our hours because we are afraid. Some writers spend their entire lives at this, rather than ever commit to putting words on the page. I didn't want to be one of those guys, so early in my career I came up with this handy motto:

Procrastinate Later

And that was helpful, it really was. It reminded me to start my writing day with the writing and save the screwing around for afterward. No two words advanced my practice of writing more swiftly and surely than "procrastinate later." They might do the same for you. But they only solve half the problem, because they don't do much at all when the whole writing paradigm breaks down and we find ourselves sort of just staring at the screen, lost. It's called writer's block, and every writer I've ever met has had it at one time or another. If you're not among that number then you are unimaginably blessed. For the rest of us, writer's block is a thicket, and it would be useful if we could find our way out. Fortunately, the path is marked in just two words:

Don't Write

Wait, what? Don't write? How can not-writing possibly solve the problem of not being able to write? Isn't not-writing exactly the issue? What the hell has Vorhaus been smoking?

Vorhaus has been smoking nothing. Vorhaus knows that writer's block takes place at the intersection of *too much fear* and *not enough information.*

Too much fear: When a creative problem gives us difficulty, we naturally start to worry that this is a problem we can't solve. Maybe it's a joke that eludes us, a snarled plot twist, or an emotion we only imperfectly understand; whatever, it walks us to the brink of our creative ability and leaves us staring into the void. At which point, apprehension becomes albatross: a weight around our necks. It keeps us from writing – literally stops us cold – because how can we think effectively when we're under this dark, glowering cloud of self-doubt? We become caught in a negative feedback loop, and that's what writer's block really is: not the absence of words, the presence of fear.

Not enough information: Interestingly, the thing that triggers this vicious circle is often just not knowing enough about the problem we're trying to solve. We haven't sufficiently stoked our inner engines with the right kind of data. Maybe we need more research about the world of our story. Maybe we need to deepen our understanding of our characters. Maybe we need to broaden our search for story beats. Maybe we just need to go deeper into ourselves and our "inner data," and figure out what the heck we're trying to say. Whatever information we're lacking, it's the lack of information that stops us cold.

So now here you are at the intersection of too much fear and not enough information. And that's when you get to follow the radical advice, *if you can't write, stop trying.* Go gather data instead. Writing, you see, is a creative act. It engages our ego, which stalls our progress. Information gathering, on the other hand, leaves the ego quite alone, because information gathering is easy; there's no fear of failure. Therefore, when writing is hard but harvesting data is easy, don't do the hard thing, do the easy thing instead.

Now watch the magic happen. Watch information-gathering relax your mind, and set you outside your fear. Watch information-gathering yield not only new data but also a more effective (because less fearful) approach to processing that data. Watch information-gathering lull your ego to sleep, so that you can start chewing once again on the creative problem you're trying to solve. Next thing you know, you're writing again. Simply, efficiently, effectively, automatically. And all because you made the decision not to write when writing was hard to do.

Let's make it step-by-step, shall we?

1. Recognize that you are blocked. (How will you know? Duh, you're not writing.)

2. Stop trying to force your way past the block. (That will just yield yucky results and make you feel worse.)

3. Go gather some information. (Seek both external and internal data sources. Sometimes the answers are already in your head and you just need to pull them out.)

4. Relax your brain. (Your ego stops tormenting you because, hey, any ol' ego can gather data.)

5. Find yourself back writing again. (Yay.)

6. Repeat as necessary. (And it will be necessary; new problems always lie ahead.)

So there you go. Writer's block sorted, forever and ever, amen. Don't thank me, I define myself through service.

Levels of Conflict

Of course there's more to solving sitcom problems than just disengaging the ego. Sometimes the problem we're trying to solve won't solve because it's either too broad or too vague. In such situations, what we want to do is break the big, amorphous problems down into smaller, more specific problems, and keep breaking them down until we get to one we can actually solve.

For instance, many people will tell you that sitcom stories need conflict. They will be right, of course, but they're not saying what *kind* of conflict. Breaking this particular problem down into its component parts, we come to understand that sitcoms contain three levels of conflict: global conflict, local conflict, and inner conflict, and that the best, most sophisticated situation comedies embrace and engage all three levels.

- GLOBAL CONFLICT is the character's war with his world. The enemy here can be anything from cops to snowstorms to landlords to rats. The essential characteristic of global conflict is that while the character cares passionately about the conflict, the enemy has no emotional investment in the character.

- LOCAL CONFLICT is direct interpersonal war between people who have a genuine emotional stake in one another's lives. Parents and children, husbands and wives, lovers, co-workers, roommates and cellmates all routinely engage in local conflict. Their lives are intertwined.

- INNER CONFLICT is the character's war with himself. This can manifest itself as self-doubt, as conflicting desires, divided loyalty or confusion about life's big questions. Anything that makes the character feel uneasy is inner conflict, and it's here that the real richness of situation comedy lies.

Let's see how this plays out on the level of story. Pretend we have a sitcom called *Family Tree* (Why not? We've had *Family Matters, Family Ties, Family Guy, Family Affair* and family every goddamn thing else.) The dad, Chet, is ordered to an out-of-town business meeting on the very weekend that his daughter, Ophelia, is singing in the school play. Here are the levels of conflict:

- GLOBAL CONFLICT: Chet's bosses don't care about Chet's family obligations, they just want Chet at that meeting.

- LOCAL CONFLICT: Chet wants Ophelia to let him off the hook, but Ophelia wants Chet to feel guilty.

- INNER CONFLICT: Chet is caught between divided loyalty to his job and his daughter.

Having broken our problem down to just these three pieces of information, we can now predict many, many scenes of the episode. There will be the scene where Chet gets the news about the meeting, the scene where he breaks the news to Ophelia, the scene where she gets angry, the scene where he tries to stand up to his bosses, the scene where Chet and Ophelia reach a meeting of the minds, and probably, God help us, the scene where Ophelia sings. That's most of the story right there, derived from just a brief glance at levels of conflict. And you can make up stories all day long using this very, very simple tool.

- GLOBAL CONFLICT: Chet is bent out of shape because the paper boy never throws the paper on the porch. (It's global conflict because the paper boy doesn't give a rat's ass about Chet.)

- LOCAL CONFLICT: Chet wants satisfaction from the paperboy, but Chet's wife, Mirabelle, thinks Chet is being petty and should just let the thing go. (The local conflict is driven by a difference of opinion on how Chet should behave.)

- INNER CONFLICT: Chet wants to have his revenge on the paper boy but doesn't want his wife to find out. (Inner conflict pits Chet between two strong, opposing desires.)

Notice how in this example the global conflict creates the local conflict and the local conflict in turn drives the inner conflict. It doesn't have to be this way – you could just as easily start with an interesting inner conflict and build it out from there. You will find that one level of conflict almost always suggests the others. Try it and see. Take a fresh look at some sitcom stories you've been working on and break them down to their levels of conflict. Then when you're done with that, use this template to make up some new stories for your show. This will yield all sorts of creative fruit and make you feel super-clever as well.

Lines of Conflict

Lines of conflict are the specific ways in which characters wage interpersonal war. Usually these battle lines are drawn along strongly opposite points of view such as liberal versus conservative, orderly versus chaotic, rule maker versus rule breaker, or about ten other examples you can probably think of now.

The best lines of conflict are broad, deep and enduring. In *Cheers,* Sam and Diane launched their intellectual class warfare upon their first meeting, and it never went away until Diane went away. On *Friends,* Ross and Rachel fought their war on many different battle grounds, but it was never anything other than Ross and Rachel's war. (It even had its own battle cry: "We were on a break!") If you're building a sitcom from scratch, and you want to make sure that it's a sturdy one with "legs" – the potential for longevity – you'll want to pay attention to the characters' lines of conflict; you'll want them to be plentiful and strong.

Suppose you have a happy, loving couple – the Palindromes, Bob and Hannah – who share the same values, goals and opinions. They adore and support each other, and want nothing but to be together. We're happy for Bob and Hannah, but we're not sanguine about their sitcom's success because, hey, what are they going to fight about? Now let's put Bob and Hannah through a divorce. Suddenly they have everything to fight about, from visitation rights to who gets custody of the Beatles CDs. And suddenly they can give us lots and lots of stories. Why? Their relationship is defined by the strong and enduring line of conflict, *divorcing couple cannot get along.*

Let's play a little fill-in-the-blank, looking at sitcom couples and defining their lines of conflict. I'll start off, then kick it to you. (At this point we're getting into the realm of real exercises, and I really recommend that you have a whack at them. You'll get much more out of this text if you do.)

- COUPLE: Sam and Diane on *Cheers*
- CONFLICT: Intellectual class warfare

- COUPLE: Al and Peg Bundy on *Married... with Children*
- CONFLICT: Lazy husband versus demanding wife

- COUPLE: Sheldon and Leonard on *The Big Bang Theory*
- CONFLICT:

- COUPLE: Frasier and Martin on *Frasier*
- CONFLICT:

- COUPLE: Jim and Dwight on *The Office*

- CONFLICT:

- COUPLE: Steve and Susan on *Coupling*
- CONFLICT:

Obviously you'll have some trouble with this exercise if I happen to mention a show you don't know, so now just pick your all-time favorite sitcom and map the lines of conflict between and among all the main characters. I'll bet good money (or even US dollars) that if it's your all-time favorite sitcom, it has lines of conflict as far as the eye can see.

Next try using this tool on characters of your own. Identify pairings that have natural enmity, like bitter siblings or divorced couples or squabbling work mates. You can also string strong lines of conflict along wildly opposite points of view. This would be your Archie and Meathead or your Dharma and Greg, and don't look down your nose at the obvious choice; those are some strong-ass lines of conflict. Go ahead and create some fresh pairings now.

- COUPLE:
- CONFLICT:

- COUPLE:
- CONFLICT:

- COUPLE:
- CONFLICT:

- COUPLE:

• CONFLICT:

You'll find the most rewarding lines of conflict in points of view with deep emotional roots. An overprotective father versus a rebellious daughter, for instance, will yield rich interpersonal conflict because, purely on the level of feeling, there's so much at stake for them both. You'll also find this to be a great way to test your prospective sitcoms or sitcom characters. If you can easily identify strong and enduring lines of conflict you can be confident that you're digging a hole in the right place.

Set Glue

What keeps sitcom characters together? Over and over again it's money. *Roommates don't have enough dough to live on their own so they have to share space.* Over and over again it's blood. *People are in the same family and live under the same roof.* Over and over again it's work. *Colleagues need their jobs, so they have to try and get along.*

Are you yawning now? I'm definitely yawning now.

The thing that holds sitcom characters together *and* makes them interesting is *set glue,* the strongest substance known to man. Set glue is *I'm right and you're wrong and we're going to stay right here together and fight about it until you agree that I'm right and you're wrong and what do you think about that?* When you've got two characters committed to that same goal, you've got yourself some industrial-strength set glue. Better, you've got yourself a war.

This war is waged in emotional spaces. When you pit an innocent character against a cynic, you have two people who are, essentially, trying to sell each other on their point of view. A win for each of them is to bring the other around, and the more strongly opposed each is at the start, the more rewarding that victory will be.

I hate to keep coming back to *Cheers* because it aired so long ago; however, it has stood the test of time, and set glue is one reason why. Diane didn't work in that bar for the money. Realistically, she could get a much better job any time she liked. No, she stayed because she desperately wanted to prove Sam wrong. And he let her stay because he wanted to prove her wrong back.

So when you're setting up your sitcom situation, think past the money. Think past the family bonds or the fact that all your characters punch the same time clock. What's really at stake for them? What are they trying to prove? Ask that of each of your characters and you'll discover something fundamental about who they are and how they fight. Go ahead and do that now.

Are you having fun with the exercises? I always consider "exercise" to be a bit of an unfortunate word. That makes it sound like work. But this isn't work, this is profoundly fun play. This is using imagination to answer a question. So let's not call them exercises. Let's call them *funnercises*. No, you're right, I can't bring myself to call them funnercises either. We'll keep calling them exercises, but we'll understand them to be play, not work.

Character Keys

When I first meet your characters, I want to know two things.

1. How will they act?

2. How will they be funny?

And I want to know right away. It's not that I'm wildly impatient to start enjoying your show (though I am). Rather, I figure that if you can't make your characters funny and interesting in the first moment I meet them, you're probably not going to have much luck later on. (And if you think I'm being uncharitable in this, at least I can tell you why; the inarticulate reader or viewer will simply say, "This sucks," and move on elsewhere.) What I'm looking for is an explosive little package that will not only make me laugh but also make me say, "Okay, I get this. I see why this will be fun."

That package is called a *character key*.

Let's say you're trying to sell me a misanthropic bartender. You think this might be funny because, you know, bartenders are supposed to be such empathetic listeners. And I think you might be right, but you're still gonna have to prove it to me. You're going to have to walk me into that bar and show me that bartender being his grumpy old self up in some customer's face right away. Don't waste time, jump right in.

Uhm, jump now. This is a funnercise.

Or you're trying to establish a character who's a ditzy blonde. You show her a sign on a door that says *push*, and she pushes. On the other side it says *pull*, so she pulls. She gets terribly confused and stays there going back and forth through that door all day. That's a character key. That's a character I get.

I'm not going to go all English teacher on your ass, but there's a word for this, *synecdoche*, the part standing in for the whole. As you introduce me to your characters, introduce each one with a good, solid slice of comic synecdoche. Give me one of their signature moves. Don't be shy. I'm not that tolerant. I'm waiting to be sold, but I won't wait long. This is called *proving it on page one*. It's something the best sitcom writers can do, and it's something all sitcom writers should aspire to. A character saying hello and giving us his name is not a character key. A tragically clumsy character overturning a table full of priceless family heirlooms is.

What are some possible character keys for the characters you're working with now (or the ones you just invented)? *Funnercise!*

If you're having trouble wrapping your mind around the mechanics of character keys, ask yourself some simple questions. How does a dumb person use a smart phone? How does a coward cross a busy street? How does a skinflint respond to a beggar? How does a rude beggar engage a skinflint? If you have a clear understanding of your character's point of view – his comic perspective – you should have no difficulty with this. A *conflict avoider* will tackle a problem at the office by diving under her desk. And if you show us her caboose, it's 100 percent guaranteed to be funny.

Rule of comedy: keisters are always funny. And I'm not just being flip here. Asses are funny because everyone has one and everyone, to one degree or another, feels self-conscious about theirs. (Mine's a little on the flat side and I have this surgery scar...) It's fundamental to funny that "comedy equals truth plus pain." The truth of the ass is *we all have one,* and the pain is *we all suffer ours.* This is so fundamental to the fundament that I invented a word to describe it: *derrierier*; more assive.

Five Ways to Be Funny on the Page

Let's cleanse the palate for a moment with some quick and dirty strategies for being funny on the page. I'm not talking so much about cracking jokes as I am about driving comic ideas through the filter of your characters' viewpoints. To test these strategies, just pick one of your favorite comic characters or sitcom scenes and see if you can generate laughs by any or all of the following means:

- DEFEAT OF EXPECTATION: When your audience or your character expects something to happen, and something else happens instead, that's surprise. If you create a solid expectation, surprise morphs into defeat of expectation, and a solid expectation will create a solid laugh when the expectation is crushed. *A man walks into a bar. Ouch!* We expect to hear the story of the man in the bar. When we realize that he's walked into the side of the building, our expectation is defeated and, presumably, we laugh.

- EXAGGERATION: Almost everything becomes funnier when you push it to its limits and beyond. *The Big Bang Theory*'s Raj was constructed to be so shy around women that he literally couldn't speak to them. That's not normal. That's exaggerated. Therefore, that's funny.

- CLASH OF CONTEXT: Simply take something out of the place it belongs and put it where it doesn't. Remember Joey and Chandler's chicken and duck? Clash of context, straight up and down. What made it funny was that the characters themselves found it so normal.

- INAPPROPRIATE RESPONSE: This is emotional clash of context. Where a response or behavior is expected, just substitute one that comes out of left field. Imagine someone eagerly looking forward to going to the dentist because his reality filter says *pain: good!*

- TABOO: Comedy begins where tolerance ends. Make people nervous by raising taboo subjects, and they will naturally store tension. That tension craves release, and finds it in the form of a laugh. Push the limit of what people will tolerate, be it sexual humor, political correctness, hot-button social issues or whatever. You'll find fertile comic territory right there.

Was that five? Counting is not my strong suit. Nor is recycling what I've already written. For a full discourse on comic tools, complete with more examples than you can stand, plus exercises up the wazoo, check out my book *The Comic Toolbox: How To Be Funny Even If You're Not.*

See How They Run

I'm going to tell you something now that's going to make you so happy. If you're developing a new situation comedy, you don't have to write characters descriptions. Does that surprise you? After all, those character sketches seem like a reliable way to discover who your characters are or to share that information with others. The thing is, though, character sketches don't really tell us who your characters are – they tell us who your characters were. *Amy grew up in Chicago. She has a degree in physical therapy. She practices krav maga.* And even if you say things like, "Sometimes she feels like an angoraphobe in a wool works," that gives us a static presentation (and maybe a dim laugh). That's your opinion of Amy. I want to make up my own mind. I want to see what she does.

And what's more, you do, too. Because discovering character through story is more efficient, more revealing, and a hell of a lot more fun than writing a thousand words on how they dress or what's their favorite drink. This is why I ask things like, "How does your character cross a busy street?" Maybe you don't know. Maybe you know nothing about your character bar her name. But if you set her down on a busy street corner, now suddenly she has a goal (get to the other side) and obstacles (traffic), and ladies and gentlemen that is a story. How your characters meets this challenge, or any challenge, tells us worlds more about them than their political leanings, where they went to school, or how they feel about cats.

Try it and see. Create a character, or use one you've recently invented, set him a challenge and have him overcome it. I'll go first.

> *A nerdy professor wants to impress a cute student. (Don't worry, they're both adults.) He tries to handle his nerdy fountain pen in a cool manner, but accidentally gets ink all over his shirt. By the time he's gotten it all over her shirt, too, we're pretty sure that she's not going to want to see him after class.*

Wow, just look at all the things I know about this guy that I didn't know before. He's self-conscious and awkward. He's bad with his hands. He makes a bad situation worse. He wants love. Holy smoke! Now I know his point of view (nervous) and how he'll be funny (by being ungainly). I know his long-term goal (to find love), and what he's going to do next (try to date the student.) That's a trove of information gleaned from just a few simple sentences. Sentences, I might add, that were more entertaining to write and more entertaining to read than any character sketch since the dawn of time. Story... simple story... is a foolproof tool for discovery. It's always there and it's always ready to serve. See for yourself. Throw a character into something, anything, and tell us what he does. *Funnercise!*

Now I have to warn you, there's a couple of pitfalls here. One is that you can get so caught up in making the story work, making it *perfect*, that you get all bogged down in detail and become unhappy. The other is that you might fall in love with these discovery tales, so that when it comes time to write real stories for your real episodes, you won't be able to let go of these first tentative, coltish, waiflike ideas. The solution to both problems is the same.

Just Don't Care

At this level of development, you're not writing stories for keeps, you're just writing stories to explore. You're trying to figure out who your characters are, how they behave, how they're funny, and why they're of interest to you. So use this technique of putting characters into story to learn what there is to be learned. *And then throw those stories away!* They've served their purpose. They told you some things about your characters that you didn't know before. Later you'll tell yourself other stories that will tell you other things. Some of those things will contradict what you thought up first. That's why you throw the first stuff away, so that it can't get in the way of what comes next. You never want past creativity to block future development.

This is actually very important. If you don't throw stuff away, it just accumulates and quickly kludges up your creative process. So here's what you need to remember: *Every level of development is just a platform upon which we stand to reach the next level of development.*

Once you've passed a level, you need never look back, and you sure don't need to cart around any kind of loyalty to those early experiments. They told you what you needed to know. Set them aside and move on.

So, well, there you have it. If you want to know who your characters really are, forget those laborious character descriptions. Forget the bibles and biographies and backstories. Just put your players in motion and see how they run. Confront them with problems and make them make choices. That's how you learn what makes them tick.

The Law of Kevin

I discovered the *Law of Kevin* late in the last century while running a comedy writing workshop in Switzerland. Now, the Swiss are not a notoriously funny people, and it turns out that they know it. So there was a lot of self-doubt in that room as we began. "Don't worry," I told them. "I know you're self-conscious. I know you don't think you can be funny. But I'm a professional, and I'm here to tell you that if you work hard and dare to dream, some day I can make you as funny as the Germans."

Ba-dum-tsh.

I guess I did my job, because it wasn't too long before a couple of newly empowered writers got into a verbal fisticuff over whose joke was better. I let them go at it for awhile before stepping in to make the point that each writer was promoting his joke mainly because it was *his joke.* Their ego investments had made them each blind to the quality of the other's idea. They had, in other words, fallen in love with their words, a very common occurrence in every writers' room in the known universe — except possibly in Switzerland, for my observation was met with blank stares. I realized that I needed to make a clearer case, so I called both writers to the whiteboard at the front of the room.

"What's your name?" I asked one. He answered with something unpronounceable and heavily umlauted, so I said, "I'll call you Kevin." I turned to the other and said, "You're Kevin, too. Now I want you both to write your name on the board." This they did, and then I asked them each to tell me in all candor which version of the word they liked best. Of course each picked his own. And there you have it, folks, the Law of Kevin:

Writers Fall in Love With Their Words
Because *They Are Their Words*

We fall in love with our words. We do. Even when it's something as neutral as a name. *Even when it's not our name!* Our words are our babies. Naturally we think that our babies are the cutest. God forbid we should have to let them go.

But if there's anything to this notion of platform thinking – that each level of development is merely a platform upon which we stand to reach the next level – then precious attachment to our words can only get in the way. This attitude is particularly noxious in a brainstorming session or a table reading, where passionate over-defense of jokes or ideas is really just over-defense of ego. It's death to the room. Here's my advice. Don't kill the room. Kill Kevin instead.

Any time find yourself fighting over a joke or resisting the natural growth you know your story demands, just tell yourself that Kevin must die.

When you find others blocking progress, tell them, too: "Kill Kevin." Share this amusing anecdote if you wish, or just don't bother. What's important is not the name of the law (though of course I'm in love with it since I named it). What's important is establishing a creative workspace where ideas freely and fruitfully advance and evolve. "Kill Kevin" is really just shorthand for, "Look, I know you think that's a pretty good joke, and maybe it is, but I see a couple of reasons why we can't use it here, including the fact that we've already used it two other places in the script and you might think that's callback but really it's just tired so we're going to have to move beyond that but we can't move beyond it until you let go of your pathological need to be the brightest, rightest, funniest voice in the room, which, by the way, nobody really cares about except you, we all just want to finish the job and go home."

See why we use the shorthand?

I wonder how we can do an exercise that will allow you to kill Kevin. Maybe try this: Have someone you trust read your script and put a check mark by all the funniest jokes. Then yank out each and every one of those funniest jokes and replace them with something else. Note that I didn't say "something better." Just something else. You'll find that the replacements are generally better, simply because they have the experience of the original jokes to draw upon – they have that platform to stand on – but that's really not the point. The point is to learn to let go. You're better off without Kevin, trust me.

The Window Idea

The flip-side to falling in love with your precious Kevins is being so overwrought or fretful that you dare not even pitch an idea or a joke to the room. This is bad for a couple of reasons. First, it might actually be a useful idea, and if you're afraid to put it out there, its utility will never be known. Second, if you're in a co-creative environment – on the writing staff of a sitcom, say – you're expected to carry your weight. If you don't contribute, you'll engender resentment, and that can't be good, can it?

Still, it's hard to give voice to an idea you don't trust or a joke you haven't tested. What if they don't laugh? What if they don't like? Then you must surely experience ego death, and a nasty, messy death at that. So naturally you want to protect yourself, communicate to your peers that this idea of yours isn't intended to be fabulous, but just something that facilitates further exploration. Wouldn't it be nice if you had a way to protect yourself here? It just so happens I have three.

- JUST THE IDEA I'M HAVING NOW: If I'm pitching an idea or a joke I'm not sure of, I preface it with, "This is just the idea I'm having now." This statement sets appropriate expectations. I state, for the record, that my idea isn't a particularly good one or bad one, just the current one. In the shorthand of my writers' rooms, it's understood that such ideas are intended to keep the discussion going forward and nothing more. That keeps my ego safe.

- THE BLIND DATE PARADIGM: In some class somewhere, I was teaching this concept of facilitating discussion through bad ideas, and a student said, "Oh, it's like going on a blind date." I had no idea what she meant, so I articulately replied, "Huh?" "Yeah," she explained, "he might be horrible, but he could have a cute roommate." That's actually a pretty sophisticated thought. You often have to pass through the bad idea to get to the good one, and if you're not brave enough to voice the bad idea, you never get to meet the cute roommate.

- THE WINDOW IDEA: In a writers' room in Sweden, we often invoked the window idea, but not in the sense of opening the window to let in some fresh air, nor in the sense of looking out the window to gain a fresh perspective. Here's what we meant when we announced a window idea: "The next words out of my mouth are going to be so horrible that I'm going to want open the nearest window and hurl myself out." No one can hold anything against you when

34

you're already holding it against yourself
so hard.

The thing is, you really need such strategies in order to keep ideas flowing freely. It's natural for egos to become engaged, and it's natural for people to clam up if they think their ideas are going to get stomped upon. By building a common vocabulary of expectation-reducing language, you build a common spirit of cooperation and collaboration. That's how you have an effective co-creative experience.

When you think about it, sitcom writers are like dogs. We travel in packs, establish hierarchies, and crave approval (and treats). A sitcom writer pitching a story or a joke is like a dog on his back in submission position. He wants to be scratched, but fears to be kicked. Be kind to your peers. Don't kick, scratch. It's just healthier all the way around.

Make Them Make Choices

Choices define characters. Not just in character exploration but in serious story development, if you really want to find out what your imaginary folks are made of, don't just put them in action, put them in a bind. *Make them make choices.* Choices are the key to everything.

Say we're back with the Palindromes, Bob and Hannah, and Bob's old girlfriend comes to town, looking to pick up where she left off. Will Bob tell Hannah, or keep this little secret to himself? As you can imagine, his choice will not only define Bob for us but also define the next beats of the story. Let's do a couple more of these to clarify the concept. I'll do mine while you do yours.

- *An office worker could rat out a co-worker and gain a plum assignment. Will he hold his tongue or let it wag?* That's a choice.

- *A mother reads her daughter's diary and finds scary news. Does she confront or conceal?* That's a choice.

- *A surly bartender is challenged to be nice to all customers for a week. Will he accept the challenge or not?* That's a choice.

Story is choice. Really it is. It's not plot mechanics. It's not about blowing things up. It's not even about great jokes, no matter how plentiful and riotous those jokes may be. It's about sending a character on a journey, driving him through choices, and seeing where he arrives. If you really want to engage your readers or viewers, if you want them solidly along for the ride, give them characters who face intriguing choices, and then make those characters choose. Not to put too fine a point on it, choices make stories worth telling.

What's it gonna be, Will Turner? Are you going to cower out and be a law-abiding citizen, or man up and be a pirate like Jack Sparrow? (Man up.) And how about you, Alan Harper? Are you going to man up and move out of brother Charlie's house or cower out and continue to sponge off of him? (Cower out.)

As we've already demonstrated, characters are defined by the choices they make. It's the job of each sitcom story, then, to show your audience something new and interesting about your characters. And you do this through the simple metric of making your characters choose.

Take a look at the sitcom you're writing now. Are your characters making choices? I don't care if they're good choices or bad choices – sitcom characters make hilariously bad choices all the time – I just want to know that there's choice involved. Because without choice there's no story, and without story there's just, uhm, this blank space here.

Fifteen Steps to
a Sitcom Story

Wow, JV, fifteen, that's a lot of steps. Where are you taking us now?

Well, you know, I've been prattling on about choice, and I thought it would be handy if I could give you a template or a story-structure map you could follow, just to see how many choices a typical sitcom character makes, why those choices are important, and what those choices reveal. So let's have a peek at a hypothetical sitcom called *Next Stop,* a coming-of-age tale about a group of friends, well, coming of age. We'll focus here on the imaginatively named Kevin, newly moved in with this group of friends and determined to free himself from his domineering mother's control.

I'm going to give you the numbered story beats that tell you abstractly what's going on, and then the way those beats are executed in this particular tale. If you're thinking ahead, you can probably predict an exercise where I give you the abstract beats and ask you to fill in the blanks on your own.

1. The character feels okay about something.

*Kevin phones his mother every day and sees
no problem with that.*

2. Something happens that makes him feel
not okay.

Kevin's friends mock his lack of independence.

3. He decides to do something about it.

*Kevin resolves to stop calling his mother every
day.*

4. He makes an attempt.

Kevin resists phoning his mom.

5. The attempt fails.

Kevin breaks down and calls mom.

6. The character tries a different approach.

Kevin disables his cell phone.

7. But this attempt also fails.

*Kevin borrows a stranger's phone and calls
home.*

8. The character makes a big, wrong choice.

*Kevin resolves to go cold turkey and cut off all
contact with his mom.*

(ACT BREAK)

9. The character enjoys temporary benefits
from the bad decision.

Kevin revels in his new-found independence.

10. The bad decision breaks down.

Kevin's mother shows up at his flat.

11. A confrontation begins.

Kevin's friends defend Kevin's independence against his mother.

12. The character appears to be losing.

Kevin fears that he has just traded one dependence for another.

13. The character makes a right choice.

Kevin rejects the influence of both his mother and his friends.

14. The character learns something new.

Kevin understands that he can think for himself.

15. And back we go to square one.

Kevin calls his mother the very next day – not because he has to, but because he wants to.

Did you notice where the act break came? That's not to make room for advertisements – they make room for ads wherever they damn well please these days. The act break is a structural choice, not a commercial one. It comes just after the character makes a big, bad choice, and you know that the consequences of that choice will have to be faced, just on the far side of the break. You could say that this is the story's "moment of maximum dread," but most people just say act break, so you can, too.

And what about these fifteen steps? Is fifteen some sort of magic number, the *da Vinci Code* of situation comedy? No. It just happens to be the number of beats in this particular story. It's a sufficient number – clearly there's enough story to fill a half-hour of television time – but it's arbitrary. How many story beats should your story have? The answer is... enough. Can I tell you that this is something you don't have to worry about? After you've developed even a handful of episodes, you'll quickly acquire the knack for knowing whether you have the right amount of story, or too much or too little. As Phillip Henslowe assures us in *Shakespeare in Love,* "Strangely enough, it all turns out well. Why? I don't know. It's a mystery." Mystery it may be, but the problem is easily solved: Start telling your story, keep telling it until it's over, and then stop.

How many choices should your character make? Again, the answer is... enough. As long as she's lurching from choice to choice and problem to problem, everything is hunky-dory. Nor do you have to put those choices in any specific spots, although there are three you can certainly count on being present in your tale.

- THE FIRST CHOICE: This is the initial decision that gets the ball rolling, such as Bob deciding not to tell Hannah about his ex-girlfriend's visit or Kevin's decision to stop calling his mom every day.

- THE BIG, BAD ONE: This choice, usually wrongheaded though sometimes just innocent of the facts, points to big trouble ahead. The audience knows that the story won't be resolved until this choice is undone.

- THE MOMENT OF TRUTH: Usually a sitcom character reaches a point where, per William Butler Yeats, "things fall apart; the centre cannot hold." Now the only way to resolve the problem is with a desperate declamation, "I was wrong!" Usually, fortunately, that works.

Meanwhile, did you guess that you'd get to fill in some blanks? Awesome prediction. Here we go.

1. The character feels okay about something.

2. Something happens that makes him feel not okay.

3. He decides to do something about it.

4. He makes an attempt.

5. The attempt fails.

6. The character tries a different approach.

7. But this attempt also fails.

8. The character makes a big, wrong choice.

(ACT BREAK)

9. The character enjoys temporary benefits from the bad decision.

10. The bad decision breaks down.

11. A confrontation begins.

12. The character appears to be losing.

13. The character makes a right choice.

14. The character learns something new.

15. And back we go to square one.

Now you have a template you can use to build your sitcom stories. It's not the only one there is, but it's one that works, so have at it.

Theme

Since we're speaking of wrong choices and right choices, we should take a moment to discuss what that means in terms of both story and philosophy. You may not know it now – might not discover it for years – but it turns out that your philosophy is every bit as important as your craft. Or let's put it this way: It doesn't really matter how cleverly you say stuff if you really have nothing to say. In the early stages of your career, you might not have much of a choice. If you're a lowly staff writer on a show called *Melanie Rules,* you can be pretty sure that Melanie's point of view is going to win out in every single episode. And if you don't like Melanie's point of view – really Melanie's creator's point of view – it doesn't much matter. You'll either write, and get paid and learn and grow, or you won't write, and pretty much stay where you are.

There will come a time, one hopes, when you do get to call the shots. You'll be the one to say, "The point of this show is to mock politicians," or "The point of this show is to help people think for themselves," or "The point of this show is to watch a dysfunctional family self-destruct," or "The point of this show is to demonstrate the awesome power of love."

Or the point of this show is these other four things that you're going to list right here. *Funnercise!*

The point of the show is also known as its *theme,* and pardon me for being a bit of a pedant about this, but I want to define theme clearly, and for the record.

Theme = The Main
Instruction Of The Story

It's what you want people to learn. In the episode described above, our buddy Kevin learns to stand up for himself, and the theme of that episode is exactly that: *Stand up for yourself!*

So, weirdly, when we speak of right and wrong, we're really speaking of thesis and antithesis. If your story is going to arrive at *stand up for yourself,* it will necessarily pass through *let others boss you around.* That's the thesis and the antithesis. Find the thesis near the end of the story and the antithesis somewhere in the middle.

In tonight's episode of *Melanie Rules,* Melanie has a crush on a new boy. The theme of the episode is *share your feelings!* I bet you a hundred million dollars that somewhere in the middle of the story, Melanie will hide her feelings, and somewhere near the end she lets them out. That's sitcom storytelling, baby. It doesn't get any simpler than that.

You might be having two thoughts right now: one, "That all sounds very preachy to me;" and two, "Who am I to tell other people what to think?" Good, solid thoughts, those. To the first I would say that if your story sounds too preachy, and you don't like that, make it less so. That's not story stuff, that's dialogue stuff. But don't let go of your theme, because the theme is the spine of the story. Without it, you've just got goo, people sitting around yakking, with no clear idea of where they're going because they're not aware (or you're not aware) that they are exactly and specifically on a journey from denial to acceptance of a theme.

As to what gives you the right to tell other people what to think, well, you acquired that right – some would say responsibility – when you became a writer. Because there's two kinds of people in this world, writers and everyone else. And everyone else looks to writers to explain shit. They can't figure it out on their own, they want us to do it for them. We're the ones standing up here saying, "Hey, people, love your fellow man!" And they're the ones out there in the audience saying, "Yeah, man, that's a good idea!" Or we're the ones standing up here saying, "Hey, people, kill zombies!" And they're the ones out there in the audience saying, "Yeah, man, that's a good idea!"

The audience *wants* our instruction. They crave it. They want to know how to kill zombies. Or tell a boy they like him. Or stand up to their mother. Or fight for freedom. Or love their fellow man. Or any of a thousand other themes you could think of. So come on, writer, tell them what to think. That's why they're paying you the big bucks.

Maybe you can't think of a thousand themes off the top of your head, but I'll bet you can think of six. Start a sentence with, "Hey, people," and fill in that blank with six instructions that are important to you. These are your themes. Your most heartfelt ones will make your strongest stories because they come equipped with your passion at no extra charge.

I suppose I should tell you which themes are important to me. If I'm going to talk the talk, I'd better walk the walk.

- Hey, people, know yourself!
- Hey, people, find someone to love!
- Hey, people, surf strange waves!
- Hey, people, if it's your trip, take it!
- Hey, people, have faith!
- Hey, people, walk down the beach, pick up everything you find, and turn it into a party hat!

All those exclamation points! I must feel very excited about my themes! Well, yeah, I do. But I want to be clear about something. My themes are my themes and they're important to me, but they don't have to be yours, not at all. If you want to say, "Hey people, do unto others before they do unto you," that's fine with me.

Funny, I object less to people's choice of themes than to their phrasing. If you think your theme is *life sucks,* you're wrong. Your theme is *accept that life sucks.* Because *life sucks* is just an opinion. It doesn't tell the audience what to do. You have the power in every single story to tell the audience what to do. You don't always exercise it, or exercise it fully, but it's always there, and the sooner you recognize that, the better off as a writer you will be.

Okay, preachy sermon over. Let's move on.

The Battles and the War

Now that we know a little more about story and theme, we can start to think about individual sitcom stories in the context of a full sitcom series, and see how they fit together. Because Melanie has been giving us such fine service recently, we'll continue to use her here, but what I really want you to be thinking about is the sitcom you're inventing, or the sitcom you plan to invent next. There's so much more to it than just stringing jokes on events like tinsel on a Christmas tree. There's the overall theme of the series you're creating, and then there are the individual themes of the stories you're telling. And these things taken together comprise the battles and the war.

So what's the theme of the show you're working on now?

Let's say that the theme of *Melanie Rules* is *grow up*. Now we know something about Melanie that we didn't know before: She needs to grow up. Won't knowing this one thing help us to drive a whole dang bunch of stories? You bet your writers' guild membership card it will. And each one of those stories is a battle in the war of Melanie's urgent and ongoing struggle to grow up. Now we have the tools to start developing one-line story ideas – pitches, yeah? And we have a tool to test those ideas. We don't have to ask *is this a good idea or a bad idea?* We can ask the much more useful question, *does this connect to the theme?* If the answer is yes, we have a story we can develop. If the answer is no, we've learned what no looks like, and that's useful, too.

Which of these stories resonates of the theme *grow up?*

- Melanie misuses her new driver's license.
- Melanie goes to the movies.
- Melanie has her first serious boyfriend.
- Melanie breaks curfew.
- Melanie bakes a pie.

Oh, this is fun. I could do this all day.

- Melanie wants to have sex.
- Melanie's grandmother dies.
- Melanie breaks up with her boyfriend.
- Melanie has a cold.
- Melanie wins a prize.

The correct answers are *yes, no, yes, yes, no,* then *yes, yes, yes, no,* and *probably not* (unless she wins the prize under false pretenses and later comes clean). Why so few *no*s? Turns out it's really hard to come up with story ideas that can't help Melanie grow up *somehow*. That's how you know it's a strong theme. The story ideas come in abundance... another indicator of a concept with legs. If you have good, strong lines of conflict, plus a broad, deep theme that leads easily to story, you know you're teeing the thing up right.

I did ten for my show. Can you do ten for yours?

And I meant it when I said it's fun. What makes it fun is that *I just don't care.* I'll put any damn idea down on the page, because I never have to ask if it's a good one or a bad one. I only have to ask if it's useful. And if it's not useful, I can either set it aside or *make* it useful. (Melanie goes to the movies, but it's an x-rated one her parents have forbidden her to see. Now we're telling a story!)

And when you get all bogged down with A-plots, B-plots and C-plots, remember this: Just as there's an overall theme for a series, and then a related sub-theme for an episode, that sub-theme can be the overall theme for the episode with (the very clumsily stated) sub-sub-themes for the individual characters' stories. The theme of *Melanie Rules* is *grow up.* The theme of this episode is *take responsibility for your actions.* In this episode, Melanie blows off a babysitting gig, her brother lets the car run out of gas, and her best friend lies about drinking. Okay, that's everybody taking responsibility for their actions (or not), so that's all stories connected to the theme.

But I've never had a fetish about that. If you have a terrific A-plot that takes your character to a very funny place, rich in emotion and discovery, your B-plot can be just a lightweight problem for a secondary character, and your C-plot can be just a running gag. It's plenty. That's just plenty for sitcom.

But your A-plot should resonate of the theme of the series (and the series should *have* a theme). Not because we're all touchy-feely and preachy over here, but just because we need that in order to tell a good story containing the fundamental building blocks of story: beginning, middle, end, and meaning.

The Want of a Scene

It might give you whiplash, the way I shift gears right here, but I'm going to stop talking about story for awhile and start talking about what goes on inside a scene. Sooner or later we're going to have to write the things, right? So we'd better start figuring out what each scene is meant to do, and how we get it to do that.

One way of understanding a scene (as we'll see, there are a few) is to ask, *What is the "want" of this scene?"* What does it seek to accomplish?

Let's say you have a character whose husband is cheating on her, and her friend has come over to reveal this startling tidbit. The want of the scene is *to try to get that information out.* What people do with it once it's out, that's another matter. The central question of this scene is, *Will the information get out?* Notice that you don't *have* to get the information out, but you have to have somebody try. Otherwise, why are you writing this scene?

And by the way, if that doesn't sound particularly hilarious – "Doris, your husband is cheating on you" – dramatic scenes need "wants" as much as comic scenes. More so, in fact, because they don't have jokes to fall back on. So understand that this concept – the want of the scene – will be with you now for as long as you write, no matter what you write. It's as fundamental to writing as coffee beans are to coffee.

When I'm working as an editor, reviewing story outlines or sitcom scripts, I frequently find myself asking, "What's the want of this scene?" Usually I ask that because I can't see the answer on the page, and that disturbs me. I might see people sitting around a bar slinging jokes like hand grenades, and that's all well and good, but what is this scene *about*? What is it trying to communicate, display, convey, or reveal? (Which is pretty much four ways of saying the same thing – I must be getting paid by the word.) (Drat, why didn't I think of demonstrate, expose, exhibit, bare, or present as well?)

To help you understand this, let's reverse-engineer a couple of common sitcom scenes, and see if we can puzzle out the want.

- Melanie has broken curfew. Now she's sneaking in late. But Dad is there waiting for her. What's the want?

Correct: to force a confrontation between this pair on the subject of house rules.

- Melanie's brother (we'll call him Doug) is alone with a girl in a parked car, and they might go all the way. What's the want?

Right again, to find out if they do.

- Melanie's mom has read Melanie's diary and now thinks that Melanie practices witchcraft. What's the want?

The exercise is left to the reader.

This other exercise is left to the reader: Take a look at a sitcom story or script you've written, go through the scenes and see if you can identify – oh, and write down – the want of every scene. It's a super effective way of testing whether a scene has a reason for being in your story or script. If you can't find a clear, clean want, you can probably cut the scene.

Okay, so that's how things stand from the scene's point of view. Next let's look at how things stand from the characters' point of view.

Who Wins?

A scene is neutral. A scene doesn't have a dog in the fight. A scene doesn't care who wins or loses. A scene just wants to see the conflict played out. It wants to know that conflict is happening, because conflict is God in story, and scenes worship God. (It's weird, don't ask.) The characters in the scenes, though, now they have a whole other agenda. They want to *win*. And another way of understanding a scene (as I said, there are many) is to ask two related questions.

1. Who wants what?

2. Who gets what they want?

Melanie is busted! Her father has caught her sneaking in after curfew. What did she want in the scene? To get in without getting caught. Did that happen? No. Melanie loses.

Doug is gay! He really doesn't want to have sex with this girl at all. Can she force him? Not in this physiology. Doug wins.

Melanie's mom confronts Melanie over this whole witchcraft business. She's hoping it's all a misunderstanding or a joke and... good news! It's a school project! Both win.

In a sitcom scene – in almost any story-based scene – there's a fairly limited range of possible outcomes. These are the ones I can think of.

- Somebody wins.
- Somebody loses.
- Everybody wins.
- Everybody loses.
- It's a draw.
- The outcome is deferred.

If you can think of other possible outcomes, go write your own darn book. (Not seriously. Send them to johnvorhaus@yahoo.com.)

Now let's look at some scenes and write possible resolutions according to the outcomes listed above. I'll do it once, then set up a couple for you.

The scene: Melanie and George (oh, did I forget to tell you the dad's name is George?) are doing homework together. Melanie wants George to do the work for her.

- Melanie wins: George does Melanie's homework.
- Melanie loses: Melanie has to do her own damn homework.
- Both win: Father and daughter bond poignantly over homework.
- Both lose: Father and daughter have a horrible fight, very Jerry Springer.

- It's a draw: They do equal amounts of homework.
- The outcome is deferred: They'll do the homework later.

The scene: Melanie and Doug both ask to use the car on the same night. What are the possible outcomes?

The scene: Melanie wants to borrow money from Doug. What are the possible outcomes?

Now grab a scene from one of your stories or scripts and chart the possible outcomes apart from the one that's already there. Don't worry about sending your story off in some skew direction; this is just a thought-exercise.

A lot of times, outcomes in a scene are dictated by what happens in the next scene or the one after that, or where the story ultimately leads. Suppose poor Melanie gets invited to the prom by a nerd. Now you know and I know that Melanie's gonna end up at that prom with that nerd because it's that sort of show. So what happens in the scene where he first asks her to the prom? Of course she says no. If she says yes now, then there's no opportunity for her to change her mind later and do the right thing. In this scene, then, Melanie wins. Well, she thinks she does. She doesn't have to go to the prom with the nerd. Later, she'll realize how hurtful she's been (it's all part of growing up, folks), and we'll understand that the only satisfactory resolution to this story is that they both win. She goes to the prom with the nerd, elevating his social status, yet somehow managing to have a good time and raise her own status as well. Ah, sitcom. So many happy endings.

Happy Endings

Oh, look, I'm not mocking happy endings. Sitcoms demand happy endings. It's what the audience wants. They want to laugh a lot and leave feeling good. And you, you working writer you, you're determined to give them what they want. That's not pandering. That's making your story rewarding and fulfilling for the people who matter, the audience.

Let's be clear: You can have a bad outcome for the character that's still a happy ending for the audience. From the outset, ol' Michael Scott in *The Office* got one bad outcome after another. They're happy endings for us because we find it rewarding and fulfilling to see him get what we think he deserved. So "happy ending" does not mean *everybody always wins*. Happy ending means that the viewer walks away with a sense of satisfaction.

If you have trouble with this, it may be because you're afraid to give the audience what they want. You might be reluctant to serve up those mushy emotional moments where everyone comes to their senses and everything ends up okay. Some call these moments, derisively, *apology ping-pong*.

"I was wrong."

"No, *I* was wrong."

"I'm sorry."

"No, *I'm* sorry."

"I love you."

"No, I love *you.*"

We've seen this scene a million times and we hate it, right? Because it's so mawkish and twee. And if you want to reject happy endings, reject away. That's your right as a writer. Happy endings, sad endings, a *dues ex machina* where everyone gets run over by a truck, those are your choices, the ones you get to make. And if making choices is how characters define themselves, I can tell you for sure that making choices is what gets writers off. So revel in those.

But be realistic. If you want the audience to respond positively to you, you have to give them a reason. Maybe it's a warm and fuzzy feeling. Maybe it's a good, solid jolt of raw failure. (Can you say *Married... with Children?*) An ending is fulfilling – not happy or sad but fulfilling – if it satisfies the audience's expectations. So just create the expectation you intend to satisfy. If you want to write a happy ending show, you say, "Hey, ladies and gentlemen, come over here and see the fluffy bunny!" And then you deliver the fluffy bunny. If you want to write an arch commentary on the futility of experience, you say, "Hey, ladies and gentlemen, come over here and see the fluffy bunny," then kill the bunny. It's a choice.

Can I tell you a secret? Sitcom audiences love a happy ending. They know it's bogus, and they don't care. They want to believe that everything's eventually going to work out fine. They might not have much evidence of this in their own lives, so they look to find it on TV. You can't fault them for this. They're not bad people. They're just... audience.

Your goal as a writer is to find your audience, serve your audience, and keep them coming back for more. Surprise! You don't necessarily need to give them what you think they want. In fact, if you try, you probably won't succeed because then you *will* be pandering, and it will show. Here's what you want to do.

Keep Giving Them You
Until You Is What They Want

That's some profound shit right there. It's worth the price of this whole book. It's your way out of this whole pandering trap. Think about the stuff that interests you, stuff you're passionate about or desperate to convey. Then go looking for people who have an equal passion for hearing about that stuff. There's your audience. Speak to them. And try to speak to bigger ones as you go along.

Your sitcom doesn't have to have a happy ending. I'm just saying most of them do.

The Pivot

Meanwhile, back here at the scene, we often find ourselves getting lost. We now have some tools to help us get found – the want of the scene and the question of who wins – but you can never have too many scene-structure tools, so here's another favorite one of mine: *the pivot*.

In this context, a pivot is *a new piece of information that triggers a change of emotional state*. It works like this. A character enters a scene in a certain frame of mind. She might be euphoric, apprehensive, curious, whatever. Then, by some means or another, new information arrives. This new information transforms the character's emotional state, and the subsequent emotional state is what carries her out of the scene. By using this tool, you can easily and reliably determine how the character feels coming in, how she feels going out, and what makes her change her mind. And when you have that information, you pretty much have everything you need for the scene.

Melanie is invited to a party and she's thrilled. But then she learns that for some reason she can't go. Now she is sad. And that's the whole scene right there. Prior condition: elation. New information: she can't go. Resulting mental state:

despair. She travels from happy to sad across the pivot of new information. Anything else that happens in the scene is just filigree: the *handles* (the jokes that get you into the scene and out of the scene), the other jokes we hear along the way, and, you know, b-story stuff.

Here's a scene from *Next Stop* involving our pal Kevin. *Kevin is home alone, and bored. Then he gets a booty call from his horny ex-girlfriend. He excitedly gets up to go.* His emotional state going in is, as described, *bored.* The pivot yields new information: *hot chick wants sex.* And Kevin's resulting mental state is *anticipation.* It's so easy to understand a scene when you break it down to these fundamental pieces.

EMOTION GOING IN
PIVOT
EMOTION COMING OUT

That's a blank you can fill in all day, every day, scene by scene, until you understand the characters' state of mind in every moment as the story unfolds. And when you come across a scene that doesn't seem to be going anywhere, you now know why: no pivot; no emotional change of state. And in case you haven't figured it out by now, emotional change of state is the engine that drives story. True fact.

So now we know what a pivot is: a new piece of information that triggers a change of emotional state. You may have heard this described as a *plot point,* and that works, too. I just like *pivot* is all.

Go through your script, scene by scene, and see if you can tease out the pivots (and yes, there can be more than one pivot in a scene) and the changing emotional states. Strong pivots equal strong stories. Make sure yours are up to the task.

The Parts of the Scene

What falls out from all of this is that you can gain clarity on the scene you're writing just by assembling the pieces before you start. Here they are as I understand them.

THE WANT: We've already discussed this. What is the scene trying to accomplish? This can be anything from "preserve a secret" to "reveal a secret" and all points in between. *Melanie has a secret crush.*

WHO WINS: You will know who wins based on where the story goes following this scene. *Melanie's crush is exposed,* and Melanie doesn't want that, so Melanie loses this scene (but opens the door to the rest of the story).

THE IN-HANDLE: This is the comic beat (where beat equals piece of action) that gets us into the scene. *Melanie is thinking of funny names for her cat.*

PRE-PIVOT BEAT: This part of the scene correlates to the character's emotional state before the pivot is reached. *Melanie feels happy because she thinks her secret is safe.*

PIVOT: This is the new piece of information that triggers a change in emotional state. *The secret is revealed.*

POST-PIVOT BEAT: This part of the scene correlates to the character's emotional state after the pivot. *Melanie feels humiliated.*

THE OUT-HANDLE: This is the comic business upon which we exit the scene. *Melanie's cat has some funny names for her, too!*

This is another template you can pull out and use as a reliable fill-in-the-blank blueprint for scene construction.

THE WANT
WHO WINS
THE IN-HANDLE
PRE-PIVOT BEAT
PIVOT
POST-PIVOT BEAT
THE OUT-HANDLE

Easy? Easy as falling asleep.

The Attitude Map

If emotional change of state is the engine that drives story, then we should be able to see a relationship between the events of the story and the changing emotional states. We should be able to tell the whole story in simple terms of, *this thing happens, and it makes him feel like that*. Well, I'm willing to play that game, and I'll even give the game a name: *attitude map*. Let's see if we can map the attitudes in friend Kevin's story of setting himself free from mum.

What happens: *Kevin phones his mother every day.*

How he feels: *Tranquil.*

What happens: *His friends mock his habit.*

How he feels: *Self-conscious.*

What happens: *He decides to stop calling mom every day.*

How he feels: *Independent.*

What happens: *He tries to not call his mom.*

How he feels: *Apprehensive.*

What happens: *He breaks down and calls his mom.*

How he feels: *Weak.*

What happens: *He disables his phone.*
How he feels: *Guardedly optimistic.*

What happens: *He borrows a stranger's phone and calls mom.*
How he feels: *Full of self-loathing.*

What happens: *He decides never to phone his mother again.*
How he feels: *Scared.*

What happens: *He enjoys his new-found freedom.*
How he feels: *Euphoric.*

What happens: *Kevin's mother shows up.*
How he feels: *Busted!*

What happens: *His friends defend him against his mother.*
How he feels: *Uneasy.*

What happens: *Kevin realizes that everyone is the boss of him.*
How he feels: *Like a loser.*

What happens: *Kevin stands up for himself.*
How he feels: *Proud.*

What happens: *Kevin learns that he can think for himself.*
How he feels: *Satisfied.*

What happens: *Kevin calls his mother again.*

How he feels: *Tranquil.*

Note that there's a certain breadth to the definition of "new information." Some information comes from outside the character, but when Kevin tries and fails to keep from calling his mom, the new information, "I'm weak," actually comes from within. This inner information is not just a valid source of pivots but actually the richest one. A story really gets rolling once you have a character thinking, "Well, I used to feel like A, now I feel like B, but I'd rather feel like C, so man do I feel like D." (Though they won't think in letters. Really they won't.)

At this point you might find it useful to view an episode of a sitcom you like and see if you can backpredict its story into an attitude map. Sometimes it's hard to see the story when it's camouflaged in jokes, but a well-constructed sitcom episode (and the ones that actually make it to air are pretty well constructed) will have a simple, solid, clear structure, one that takes its characters on a specific emotional journey, making specific stops along the way. By attitude mapping such episodes, you start to get a sense of how plentiful the story beats are, and how frequently and radically the character's emotional state changes.

There's a certain amount of nuance to this. A character might be frightened in one beat of the story and apprehensive in another. Those are pretty similar emotional states, and it's okay that they are. Characters can pass through comparable emotions at different times in the story. Likewise, you needn't always be ratcheting back and forth between positive and negative states. You might have a character anticipating a future event with the feeling, *This is gonna be good.* Then he gets some new information which leads him to think, *No, this is gonna be great!* He's moved from a positive state to an even more positive state, and that's fine, too.

Can you think of a moment in one of your stories where a character goes from a negative state to an even more negative one? If you can't, can you invent one?

Man Uses Tools

I guess you're starting to see that you can look at a sitcom story a bunch of different ways. Here's why that's useful: because a lot of times, the way you're currently looking at a story doesn't help you figure it out. You get stuck. You lose track of what story you're telling, how it should evolve, what point you're trying to make, and how it might end. But now when you're lost, you don't have to stay lost for long. Now you have all these different tools you can use. If you've squeezed the attitude map dry and you still can't solve the story, go back and think about its theme. If theme avails you not, try the fifteen steps. If the fifteen steps prove worthless, play with your pivots. By these means you move away from vague and unstructured questions like, "What happens next?" and get down to your story's hard facts – its actions and emotions. You're figuring things out rationally, not randomly. There's nothing wrong with random creativity – I'll take found art wherever I can find it – it's just not very efficient is all. Tools are efficient. Tools are handy. Man uses tools. Were it otherwise, we'd still be living in trees wondering where our next banana was coming from.

Tools, however, have problems of their own. When we speak of *tool-driven creativity*, we're talking about any logical thought process or consciously-invoked strategy that abets the brain's innate ability to solve creative problems without overt guidance or control. Use a tool and you free yourself from dependence on inspiration alone. But here's the thing about creative tools: At first blush, they seem not just counter-intuitive, but actually *anti*-intuitive. Many people using tool-driven creativity for the first time fear that the use of tools will somehow hurt their natural, innate creativity. That's because at first, well, it does.

If you were first starting to use any physical tool, a spud bar, say, or a conduit bender, it would naturally feel awkward and clumsy in your hands. But then you'd master it – you'd be a spud bar stud – and that awkward feeling would go away. It's the same with mental tools. You work with them and play with them and try them and test them, and soon enough that self-conscious, paint-by-numbers feeling starts to fade.

Work with creative tools for even a short period of time, and you will soon find a change taking place. What was awkward and self-conscious quickly becomes easy and automatic. Rather than losing your innate creativity, you will ally that natural force with a new means of using it efficiently and reliably.

Tool-driven creativity, then, comes to us in phases.

- PHASE ONE: We don't use creative tools at all. We don't know what they are. We rely on instinct or trial-and-error, which may serve us reasonably well in terms of quality, but not at all in terms of quantity or efficiency. We are at the whim of inspiration.

- PHASE TWO: We start using creative tools and spend some time learning how they work. During this period, it's common to feel that our creativity has become "clockwork," and common to feel that something has been lost.

- PHASE THREE: Creative tools start to fit. Having used them for a while, we discover that we get quite a lot more creative *quantity*, and also that the creative *quality* of phase one is starting to return. With skillful mastery, creative tools become part of our natural and automatic creative process.

- PHASE FOUR: Creative tools go deep. They sink into our subconscious and become a reliable ally to our natural creative juice. More than that, they give us a way out of traps. When inspiration doesn't yield the answers we need, or we just need a fresh way of looking at a problem, tool-driven creativity is there. Thus we step outside the despair of ever having to face a problem we fear we can't solve.

No exercises for this section. Just... hang in there, and trust your tools. Once you learn to bring your toolcraft to bear on any story or script problem, you're going to find that you get more solutions, better solutions, easily arrived at and conceptually sound. You might even get more sex.

What is Comedy?

Maybe I shouldn't have waited so long to say it, but *comedy is cruelty*. A thing isn't funny to the person it's happening to. It's funny to the rest of us watching. Tell me you haven't been funny a thousand times by making yourself the butt of your own joke. *"I'm so stupid I couldn't pass a blood test."* That's you being cruel to you for the benefit of others. Seriously, that's really all you need to know about writing comedy. Find a character. Put him in a bad situation. And then make the bad situation worse. So then –

Wait, wait, hang on. I'm just sitting here wondering *why* comedy is cruelty and you know, I can't think of a good reason. I did, though, think of a joke.

> In the years before World War II, in a little Polish village, a learned rabbi used to teach his students, "Life is like the ocean." And they would nod and respond, "Yes, life is like the ocean." One young student was particularly taken with this philosophy, and he carried it with him through the long years of the war, which he barely survived. Later becoming a rabbi in his own right, he moved to Philadelphia, and

taught all his eager young students, "Life is like the ocean." Year after year, "Life is like the ocean." And they would nod and respond, "Yes, life is like the ocean." One year, though, a student asked, "But Rabbi, *why* is life like the ocean?" And the rabbi had no answer. *Why* is life like the ocean? The question haunted him. It plagued him so much that eventually he returned to his home village, hoping against hope to find his teacher still alive. Incredibly, the rabbi had survived the war, though now was quite old and in fact lay on his death bed when the young man arrived. He knelt by the old rabbi's side and entreated, "Rabbi, Rabbi, *why* is life like the ocean?" The old man looked at him through watery eyes and replied, "Okay, so life isn't like the ocean."

Now, who's getting the cruelty here? Is it the hapless young rabbi who invests his life's work in an empty premise? Or is it the reader, who expects some sort of significant payoff and gets a smirky slap in the face instead? Actually, it's both. They're two sides of a certain coin. The young rabbi gets an unpleasant surprise, while the audience gets a startling defeat of expectation.

I'll tell you one more joke to illustrate the point.

These three ducks walk into a bar. They go up to the bartender and order drinks. The bartender asks the first duck, "What's your name?" "I'm Huey." "Yeah? How's it going,

Huey?" "Not too bad, you know. Into
puddles, out of puddles, into puddles, out
of puddles all day long. Not a bad day for a
duck." Huey goes off to the bathroom. The
bartender goes to the second duck and
says, "What's your name?" "I'm Dewey."
"Yeah? How's it going, Dewey?" "Not too
bad, you know. Into puddles, out of
puddles, into puddles, out of puddles all
day long. Not a bad day for a duck." Dewey
goes off to the bathroom. The bartender
goes down to the third duck and says, "I
suppose you're Louie." "No," says the duck,
"I'm Puddles."

I'll bet you did *not* see that coming. So the
punchline defeated your expectation, but that's not
why the joke works. The joke works because of
poor Puddles. We feel his pain. And since it's *his*
pain, not *our* pain, we can go ahead and laugh.
Poor Puddles.

Now here's how this plays out in sitcom.
(Notice I still haven't said *why* comedy is cruelty.
Maybe I'm hoping you'll just let that slide.) To
delight our audience, we consistently make our
characters miserable, and to make our characters
miserable, we just invent other characters
designed to give them the worst possible time.
Let's have a peek at *Big Bang Theory's* Leonard.
From the first moment forward, who made his life
hell? For sure you're going to say Sheldon, with his
idiosyncrasies, phobias and Roommate Agreement
driving Leonard up the wall. You should also say
Penny, for while she never intentionally set out to

be cruel to Leonard, she immediately became the object of his unrequited love, and her very presence in his world brought him grief of the deepest kind by destabilizing his worldview that "the nerds are alright." You can see a similar line of grief between Howard and his unseen mom. In fact, you can fruitfully go around from character to character in that sitcom, or any successful sitcom, and make a list of who makes whom miserable and how. You will find – and it's funny to think about because sitcoms are supposed to be so light and fluffy – that misery abounds.

Notice that these lines of cruelty run in much the same directions as the lines of conflict we discussed earlier. That's not by accident. The same things that drive the narrative drive the comedy. If you have a story with lots and lots of problems for your main character, you also have a story with lots and lots of jokes, because each one of those problems will make that character suffer, and comedy is cruelty, so there you go.

I don't want to go too deep into this (I'm well over my head already) but not only do comedy and story line up together here, so does theme. This is because...

The Truth Is Revealed Under Pressure

And the truth is that no character will move from denial to acceptance of the theme – admit the truth, that is – without sufficient pressure forcing him to do so. That pressure moves the story along. *And* it generates the jokes. *And* it drives the character to a new understanding. That's some triple-duty pressure there. It's pretty marvelous stuff.

Are you worried about being cruel to your characters? Don't be. They're characters in a story. They don't really exist and you can't really hurt them. If you ever find yourself holding back, it could be a case of conflict avoidance. Many writers are conflict avoiders in their real lives. I am. You might be, too. I can't say from here, and sure don't want to get in a fight over it, but I do know that to make real people laugh, you have to make fake people ache. So if you're averse to cruelty, you'd better get over that, or you'll never be sufficiently funny on the page. Comedy is cruelty. If you want to be funny, you'd better be cruel.

So, are you still waiting for me to tell you *why* comedy is cruelty? Hey, I'm a knowledgeable guy, I should be able to pull that off. Maybe I've studied the world's great humorists: Aristophanes, Shakespeare, Twain. Maybe I've peered into the depths of my own soul and sought the answer there. Maybe I *have* found out why life is like the ocean. But you know what?

The exercise is left to the reader, ha!

Types of Sitcoms

What type of sitcom are you creating? If you reply "family sitcom" or "workplace sitcom," you've only half answered the question. Here's the rest of the answer, the basic types of sitcoms that get made over and over again, and succeed over and over again, because they work so well.

- COMIC OPPOSITES: It's the simplest comic formula. Take Dharma. Add Greg. Make sitcom. That its simple doesn't diminish its strength. Find two characters with strongly opposing points of view, lash them together with set glue – the urgent need to change each other's mind – surround them with fun secondary characters, and you've got yourself a show.

- CENTER AND ECCENTRICS: A normal character is surrounded by comic characters. This is *Scrubs*, and before you say, "Hang on, JD's not normal," I'm way ahead of you. A character isn't normal because he's not funny; he's normal because he's our surrogate, our window on the world. He's also the one the others turn to for answers. Who has the most emotional intelligence in your cast? That's your center. Everyone else has less self-awareness and more broadly comic qualities.

- ENSEMBLE: A group is united against a common enemy. The gang on *It's Always Sunny in Philadelphia* might fight against each other from time to time (all the time) but they band together against outside threats. That, plus the fact that there's no definable center to the show, makes them an ensemble. In this type of show, all your main characters have similar levels of emotional intelligent. They get roughly equivalent amounts of story time and are equally driven by the theme.

- FISH OUT OF WATER: Take a character or a group of characters from the place they feel comfortable, put them someplace new and challenging, and *voila*! Fish out of water. You could put *Weeds* in this camp, because even though Nancy Botwin was still a suburban mom after her husband died, she'd never been a pot dealer before. The world of drug dealers was the new and challenging one she entered. This is another reliable type of sitcom because it's just so darn easy to stick a character in a place she doesn't belong.

- POWERS: Mostly this is kids' stuff. Give your character a magical power and watch the hilarity ensue. The trick here is to find something that hasn't already been done to death – witches, wizards, genies, aliens, ghosts, we've seen much of this before. But if you can find a magic power that hasn't already been exploited in sitcom, you have yourself a pearl of great price.

Two exercises here. First, identify which type of sitcom you're creating. Don't be afraid to cross types; it's acceptable to mix and match. Second, what would happen if it were otherwise? Can you reconceive your sitcom as a different sort? Can you, for example, find and define a central character in your ensemble? Conversely, can you spread the emotional weight around to create an ensemble? You may not ultimately make such changes, but to make the attempt will definitely open some doors to your thinking, and give you a fresh look at your work.

The Rules of Your World

A certain kind of humor you see in a lot of situation comedies is *demonstration comedy*: jokes or funny bits put there for no other reason than to amuse the audience. Got nothing to do with story. It's just there. An example of this can be seen in "The Nerdvana Annihilation" episode of *The Big Bang Theory*. The guys bought a movie-prop time machine and were playing at time travel. While Leonard worked the prop's controls, Sheldon, Howard and Raj moved around in a jerky simulation of accelerated time. Notionally, they were doing this to make the illusion of time travel more real for Leonard, but mostly they were doing it to make us laugh.

Now, I bring this up for a couple of reasons. One is just to prove that comedy isn't always cruelty. The other is to segue into a discussion of the *rules of your world*. An excellent situation comedy makes a number of promises to the viewer, and in so doing establishes the rules of its world. You'll want to give some thought to this when you design your show, so that you make a set of promises you can reliably keep and, crucially, will enjoy keeping as time goes by.

I've seen sitcom proposals with lines like this: *Jack is a master of dialects; every week he shares a new one.* Well, not only will this bit of demonstration humor get old very quickly, it also proves a very tough promise to keep. Once you've run through Cajun, Boontling, Cockney, Kentish, Okracoke, Scouse and Geordie, where are you? Here's broader choice, more rooted in emotion than behavior: *Jack is a grammar Nazi; every week, some sort of apostrophe catastrophe freaks him out.* Now you have a joke – one rooted in character – that you can repeat for as long as language lasts.

The rules of the world cover everything you use in your show from dirty words to voice-overs. Is yours a show that addresses adult themes? Does it break down the fourth wall (acknowledge the audience's presence)? Does it mimic "real reality" or does it step off into fantasy? No show in (my) recent memory stepped off harder into fantasy than *Scrubs,* which gave us constant peeks inside John Dorian's head. It was a promise of the show – a rule of that world – that you would see JD cock his head to one side and go off into some crazy daydream. It became the heart and soul of the show – as it was designed to do from the outset.

So... it's a rule of *Melanie Rules* that Melanie rules. One way or another, each week she's going to have her way. Other rules of behavior I can predict: Doug will be a half-baked flake; George will be a concerned but ultimately indulgent father. Mom will have a name. More intrinsically, each episode will provide Melanie with a lesson;

the show will have a strong moral core. Why? Because ultimately that's the point I want to make about rules: that they don't constrain your behavior, they guide you to a higher purpose. That's what's on my mind, and I'm gonna keep giving them me until me is what they want.

Now some of these choices are arbitrary, and they will change as time goes by and the stories and characters develop. But some are so fundamental to the show – theme, settings, voice-over, levels of conflict, presence or absence of emotional truth – that it's worth laying them out at the outset. If nothing else, this effort will clarify for you what your show is or is not about.

So, what are the rules of your world? What can I expect to see in every episode of your sitcom? That list would be handy to have.

The Jobs of a Pilot Episode

There are two kinds of sitcom pilots, called respectively *the premise pilot* and *the context pilot.* A premise pilot will be a story that establishes the new reality of the sitcom world we're visiting. The first episode of *Cheers* was a premise pilot because it introduced Sam and Diane to each other and introduced us to their conflict. Likewise, the first episode of *The IT Crowd* was a premise pilot because it brought Jen into the twisted world of Moss and Roy. If I were to write the premise pilot for *Next Stop,* it would be the story of Kevin's first day in his new house with his new roommates.

A context pilot joins the story in progress. Though we will be given information that clues us into the relationships and the lines of conflict, we will be the only stranger here; everyone else will already know each other. *The Office,* in both its British and American iterations, was a good example of this. The office was established, along with its personalities, conflicts and dynamics; the only thing different was the presence of a documentary television crew. Most family sitcoms are launched with context pilots for the simple reason that most families don't just "start." They're ongoing. You could go all the way back to such classics as *All in the Family* or *The Cosby Show* to see first episodes that "join the story in progress." Probably the pilot of *Melanie Rules* will track the same way.

Which approach is better? Well, neither, per se. Each is only better as a function of how well it sets up the show and gets it running. If yours is a story of the challenges facing newlyweds (*Dharma and Greg*), then a premise pilot makes sense, because you can tell the story from the first problem forward. However, if yours is a story of the ongoing challenges facing a couple that's been married for awhile (*Mad About You*), then a context pilot is the way to go.

So that's one job of the pilot episode: to start the story. There are, ahem, a few others.

- INTRODUCE THE CHARACTERS: Use character keys to convey what each character thinks, how they act, and how they will be funny.

- ESTABLISH THE LINES OF CONFLICT: Tell us who fights with whom; demonstrate that there are solid, enduring lines of conflict that will yield solid stories for, uhm, ever.

- DISPLAY THE FUNNY: Will we have demonstration comedy? Sight gags? Verbal wit? Warm smiles or belly laughs? Intellectual humor or slapstick? Tell us what we'll laugh at when we come back and watch again.

- ESTABLISH TONE: What's the pace and tempo of the show, its level of sophistication, its depth of emotional truth?

- MAKE THE RULES: Will you have voice-overs, flashbacks, fantasy? Do the characters acknowledge the audience? Does the sitcom acknowledge the real world? These are just some of the givens you have to establish.

- ANNOUNCE THE THEME: What is the show about? Why is it important? What is it trying to teach?

- CREATE THE PROMISE: Everything we see in the pilot we will expect to see again in subsequent episodes, so make sure you're happy with what you propose.

You can probably think of other jobs for your pilot episode. Perhaps there's a running gag you want to establish, or a signature style of dialogue, like the choppy, rapid-fire back and forth used to such great effect in Aaron Sorkin's brilliant *Sports Night*. Maybe you want to telegraph that you'll be using non-linear narrative, as in Steven Moffat's equally brilliant *Coupling*. You might take a moment now and draw up a short list of the unique qualities of your show that you want to showcase. These are the jobs of your pilot episode, so make sure you do them all.

The one thing I really want to stress is: Don't make promises you can't keep. Perhaps you have decided, you Shakespeare you, to do the entire pilot episode in iambic pentameter. Maybe you even plan to come back in subsequent episodes with sonnet structure, haiku, light opera, or an uproarious take on Noh drama. Sooner or later, you're going to drive this gimmick into the ground, and then where will you be? *There once was a sitcom from Kent...*

A propos of absolutely nothing, a friend once told me he could tell how "smart" a TV show was just by the color of the sets and costumes. The brighter and more primary the colors were, the more likely was the comedy to be aimed at kids (and drunk adults), with little sophistication and much slapstick. If the colors were muted, pastel, that show was going to have more smarts, more relationship-driven conflict, and more emotion. With *Teletubbies* at one end of the spectrum and *Friends* at the other, so far I have yet to see him proven wrong.

He still can't get a job though, but whatever.

Places of Being,
Places of Doing

When you start to think about the setting of your sitcom, the places where events will actually unfold, you'll want to think in terms of *places of being* versus *places of doing*. What you're going to discover is that places of being are far more useful to you than places of doing, and you'll want to choose your settings with this in mind.

Let's think about a health club. God knows a lot of people have proposed sitcoms set in health clubs, gyms and such. But there's a problem with this setting. If you have a lot of exercise machines littering your set, people are expected to use them. There is no logical reason for them to be in that space, at least more than momentarily, if they are not *doing* that thing of working out. So in addition to figuring out your story, you're going to have to figure out plausible uses for all that gym equipment all the time. That will get old, fast. On the other hand, if you set your sitcom in the juice bar *adjacent* to the health club now you're home and dry. Why? Because people can hang out in a juice bar all day. They need no excuse to come there, and they need no excuse to stay.

Juice bar, tavern, coffee shop, café, break room, restaurant, cafeteria, kitchen, park, common workspace, living room, rooftop, back yard, patio, smoking room (smokequarium!) – these are all places of being. Why is a common workspace a place of being, not doing? After all, shouldn't these people be working? Well, yes, they should, but as the workplace cast is a surrogate family to one another, the office actually becomes a surrogate living room. Business is taking place, granted, but it's acceptable (within both the rules of the world and of conventional reality) for folks just to hang out.

Bedrooms and bathrooms, on the other hand, are places of doing (we need not dwell on doing what). Yes, you can set some scenes in places like this, but not many and not often, because there are few organic reasons for people to gather in a bedroom or a bathroom. That's why you'll see them in sitcoms occasionally, but they won't be standing sets. It's just too hard to stage the main action in a place of doing.

Needless to say, you want your standing sets to stand there. No point in devising a sitcom that's set in a different house every week. Just too expensive to shoot. So now we see that there's a unity between the premise of your sitcom and its settings. Some great premises fail to stand the weight of development just because they're impossible to present onscreen. In others, the premise and the setting are integral. I once developed a sitcom in Romania (yes, Romania) called *Antechamber*. It was set in the antechamber

– the front office – of a fictional president of Romania. There, in that one setting, the staff could work, play, love, hate, change, grow, and be hilariously funny. You almost didn't have to go anywhere else.

This consideration of cost is not for nothing. People reading and judging your scripts will want to know not just if you're brilliantly funny and hopelessly heartfelt, but also whether you're realistic. Propose a sitcom set on the moon, complete with one-sixth gravity, and you're presenting quite a production problem. Worse, you're revealing your naïveté. Adrian Lyne, the director of the movie *Jacob's Ladder,* looked at this line of scene description, "Jacob opens the door and stares into the abyss," and famously remarked, "How many carpenters will it take to build the abyss?" No abysses in your sitcom. Not as a central set. No working farms. No tollbooths. Give us places of being, and cheap ones at that. History tells us that an enduring and successful sitcom can get by with just two main sets (*The Cosby Show*), or even just one (*Cheers*). It can be done, and it demonstrates your nous when it's done by you.

The Goldilocks Setting
and the BFM

"Nous" is a lovely word. In British English it's understood to mean common sense or capability. You could use it in a British sitcom, but not an American one, because too few Americans know the word. They'd fail to get the joke you built on that word, and then feel self-conscious and dumb. Audiences that feel self-conscious and dumb tend not to stick around. On the other hand, audiences also don't stick around when the show they're watching fails to challenge them at least a little. In the former case, they don't know enough to enjoy the humor. In the latter case, I guess you could say, they know too much.

Consider this one-liner.

> *A Ukrainian is asked if he can eat a*
> *hundred pounds of apples, and he replies,*
> *"What I cannot eat I will nibble."*

I don't find this joke funny because it speaks to something about Ukrainian character that I don't know. I think it has to do with how they eat or hoard or something, but frankly I'm at a loss; I can't figure out where the cruelty lies. Well, guess what? I'm not the target for that joke. The teller isn't trying to make me laugh. He's trying to make Ukrainians, or people who know Ukrainians, laugh. Because I am neither of these things, I don't have enough information to solve the puzzle of the joke. Therefore, I don't laugh.

Here's another joke that's not funny.

Why did the chicken cross the road? To get to the other side.

This one's not funny because we've all heard it before. Humor relies on surprise, and in this case there is none. There's no challenge to our understanding, no defeat of expectation, no snappy little puzzle to solve. Therefore, we don't laugh.

So now we know that there's a relationship between information and humor. Too little information kills the joke. Too much information kills the joke as well. *The Goldilocks Setting* – the place where the joke is just right – is when the audience has enough information to solve the puzzle of the joke, unlocking its twist in a satisfying way. Try this joke on for size.

A Chukcha comes into a shop and asks, "Do you have color TVs?"

"Yes, we do."

"Great," says the Chukcha, "give me a green one."

Do you know what a Chukcha is? I do, but only because I worked for two winters in Moscow (comedy is cruelty) and learned about these indigenous Siberians whom other Russians mock as dimwits. It's the Russian equivalent of our old Polish jokes, the kind we no longer tell, thanks to political correctness – a concept that hasn't caught on in Russia yet, let me tell you. But even if you've never heard the word Chukcha before in your life, you probably got the joke. There was enough information in the puzzle to let you appreciate the twist. Hey, it's no knee-slapper, but at least the joke lands. As an audience, then, we often glean clues from context, enough to get the joke; enough to laugh. Sometimes it's the very presentation of new information that makes the joke work. Consider this one:

Not to generalize but... fucking Russians.

You need know nothing about the character of Russians to understand that the teller of the joke, at least, considers them impossible. Part of why this joke works is the release of new information, or at least opinion. "Hmm, Russians are impossible. This I did not know." Also note the tiny defeat of expectation built into the joke. Someone says, "Not to generalize..." and then proceeds to generalize. Boom! The joke lands.

Now we can see our audience as a bell curve. At the left end of the curve are people who don't get the joke because they don't have enough information to solve the puzzle. The joke is literally too smart for the house. At the right end of the curve are people who don't get the joke because they have too much information – they've heard it before, or it's so obvious that there's no satisfaction in working it out. Is there such a thing as too dumb for the house? That's what that joke would be. Your target audience, then, the people you're trying to reach and amuse, is the *BFM* or *Big Fat Middle.* Not everyone, not the whole population. Just most of them. It's not realistic to think that your jokes will work for everyone.

Note, however, that you can "tune" a joke. If there's not enough information for (most of) the audience to solve the puzzle, you can front-load the joke with additional information.

> *Alcohol may intensify effect? Great!*
> *Instructions!*

Crucial information is missing here (or maybe not entirely missing but just vaguely implied). To make this joke work better, we might say,

> *When I see the words on a pill bottle,*
> *"Alcohol may intensify effect," I think,*
> *"Great! Instructions!"*

Two things to think about here. First, don't forget about your precious Kevins. There's more than one way to tell a joke, just as there's more than one way to tell a story or solve a scene. Don't get hung up on your first solution. Always make room for the new idea, for the new idea has the old idea to draw upon, and will likely be stronger. Second, recognize that you won't always win. No matter how hard you try to tune a joke, you're going to lose both ends of the bell curve, and maybe most of the middle, too. What can I tell you? That's showbiz.

Spend a few minutes now rewriting some of your jokes. Try to kill them by providing too little or too much information. Then resurrect them by tuning them in a new and different way.

One more Chukcha joke to get out on.

A Chukcha wrote to his brother, "I heard you had a baby, but was it a boy or a girl? Am I an aunt or an uncle now?"

Those wacky Chukchi...

Skeletons

One place where sitcom writers often get stuck is in trying to make the transition from exploratory tools like the attitude map or the fifteen steps into real story outlines and scripts. Up to a certain point, you're just playing at story development. Every choice is arbitrary and every choice can be changed. Eventually, though, you need to settle on the story you're telling and figure out how to tell it effectively, in preparation for writing the script. Many writers skip this step. They take their vague and unformed ideas and try to turn them into scripts right away. To me this is problematic because you end up having to do two jobs at once.

1. Figure out your story.

2. Make it funny.

To wax metaphorical, you're trying to build walls and hang paintings on them at the same time. Nice trick if you can pull it off. I can't. I've met damn few writers who can. Most everyone I know even has trouble going from concept to story outline without freaking out. There seems to be a need for an interim step there. Once upon a time I called this interim step *premise pages,* and described it as a two-page telling of the tale, incorporating only as much detail as can be crammed into two pages. I always hated that term, though, premise pages. It was like, "Write me a premise pages." It did not fall trippingly from the tongue. For awhile I called that document a *skin*, but eventually settled on *skeleton* as a more apt term for the basic framework upon which the subsequent outline or script will hang.

So here's what a skeleton is: a two- or three-page, single-spaced, present-tense document that tells as much as you now know about what's going on in your episode. It concerns itself with two and only two classes of information.

1. Action.

2. Emotion.

Action and emotion. What happens. How people feel. That's it. Nothing more. No style, no metaphor, no snarky asides, no laborious scene descriptions, no dialogue, no jokes. If you think you know where or how an action or emotion is going to be funny, you can throw a nod to that, but only to demonstrate, to yourself or others, that you know where the funny will later go. The key word here is "later." Now is not the time to be funny. Now is the time to clarify what happens and how it makes people feel. Here's a hunk of skeleton from something I'm working on now:

> *Jim returns to his London hotel room and opens a Skype connection to his family back in Los Angeles. Viewing the kitchen of his home on his computer, he is surprised to*

see a stranger there, robbing the place. He tries to alert 911, but they think his call from London is a prank and hang up. So he writes the words, "Cops are coming!" on a piece of paper and holds it up to his webcam, frantically waving his hands to get the burglar's attention. When the burglar sees the sign and flees, Jim is relieved to have thwarted a robbery, but shaken to find himself so far from home in his family's time of need.

Later, Jim and his wife, Jill, talk about the burglary. In the course of the discussion, Jill breaks down in tears, not over the burglary but over the fact that Jim has only been gone a week and she doesn't know how she'll make it through six months of separation. Jim assures her that they'll solve their problems as they always do, with open communication and love. Deep inside, though, Jim is worried, too.

Okay, so what do we have here? Action. Emotion. A hint at the funny. Note that we can also see the want of each scene (to show the burglary; to talk about the burglary). We can see who wins (Jim in the first scene, because he drives the burglar away; neither in the second scene because they both still have anxiety). And we get the pivots (the burglar appears; Jill breaks down in tears).

Two exercises for you now. First, take a script you've already written and reverse-engineer the skeleton text for a scene or two (or even the whole thing). Next, take a hunk of an attitude map and translate it into skeleton stuff. That oughta keep you busy for a bit.

Note the use of the word "translate" there. Viewed through a certain filter (one I just happen to have handy) every step of a script's evolution can be viewed as a translation.

- The PITCH is a one-paragraph translation of the idea.
- The ATTITUDE MAP (or other tool) is a beat-outline translation of the pitch.
- The SKELETON is a two- to three-page translation of the attitude map.
- The OUTLINE is a fully developed, scene-by-scene translation of the skeleton.
- The SCRIPT is a translation of the outline into scene description and dialogue.
- The PRODUCED EPISODE is an audio/visual translation of the script.

Recalling our discussion about platform thinking, we can now see that concept in a new light. Once the episode is shot, who really cares what the script looked like? Once the script is written, who really cares what flaws existed in the story outline? Once the story outline – well, you get the idea. Each level of development is merely the platform upon which we stand to reach the next level. Once you're up there, you can ignore the scaffolding below you and continue to climb higher. Therefore, strive to make every level of development not pretty, but simply utilitarian. All any level really needs to be is something that can be effectively translated to the next level. No need to make it pretty. Just make it clear.

Here should follow a long and laborious discussion of what elements go into a right and proper story outline. But I already covered that ground pretty well in *Creativity Rules!* and if you can't be bothered to buy that whole book, just shoot me an email and I'll send you the relevant text. Here's a shorthand version of what belongs in a story outline and what does not:

- IN: Actions. Decisions. Descriptions. Intentions. Emotions. Revelations. Relationships. Backstory. Detail. Events. Surprises. Lessons.

- OUT: Stylish prose. Literary pretension. Analogy. Metaphor. Simile. Opinion. Tangents. Witticisms. Dialogue. Jokes.

What you should have when you're done is a clean, crisp version of your story in workaday English prose (unless you're writing in Urdu; then you'd want workaday Urdu prose), uncluttered by a lot of unnecessary asides (and parentheticals) (like that one about Urdu). At its best, a story outline will provide the basis for an easy translation into script. It will tell you where and when every scene takes place, and which characters are involved. It will also tell you the want and winner of each scene, plus the pivots, the emotions, the actions, and a sense of where the jokes lie. It will not cloud your thinking with meaningless pretty words or rambly asides.

Ten Random Things That Will Improve Your Work

Over there in my notebook I have some topics I haven't found a place for elsewhere. I find a place for them here.

- In sitcom, it's often a case of *first you make the mistake, then you learn the lesson.* Your character will blunder, probably lie, get himself in hot water, and then work his way out of it both by telling the truth and by achieving a new understanding. If you're having trouble getting a handle on your sitcom story, just ask yourself, "What's the mistake? What's the lesson?" and build out your story from there.

- Another tool you can use to great effect is *the pressure and response piston,* wherein everything in your story is understood as either pressure or response to pressure, and nothing else. It's a great way to make a bad situation worse. Start with a problem, have the solution to the problem create a bigger problem, try solving that one, only to create a bigger one, back and forth like, yes, a piston, until everything explodes.

- *Sitcoms are about relationships.* If you examine every action, every decision, every conflict, every outcome, every plot twist, every resolution in terms of how it affects the relationships of your characters, you won't go too far wrong. We want to be amused by a sitcom, sure, but more than that, we want to be engaged. Give us compelling relationships first, and the funny can come along at its leisure.

- *Sitcom characters are sympathetic monsters.* Sympathetic because we care about them; monstrous because their skewed point of view makes them do horrible, terrible, self-serving (or self-destructive) things. In *The Office*'s Michael Scott we find a sympathetic monster. (*The Office*'s David Brent is slightly less sympathetic and more monstrous.) We laugh; we care; the show is a hit. Are your characters sympathetic monsters? If not, go back and remake them until they are.

- Your stories must always meet the needs of both *plot logic and character logic.* Plot logic is what happens because the writer needs it to happen. Character logic is what happens because it makes sense to the characters to do it. If you serve only plot logic, your audience will feel manipulated and unsatisfied. If you serve only character logic, the story might not go where you need it to go. Attend to both, and don't be lazy. Demand of yourself that you serve both logics completely.

- There's such a thing in sitcom as the *three-dimensional joke*. A 3-D joke does three jobs: it tells a truth; it advances the story; and it's funny. Not all lines of dialogue achieve this lofty goal, but the best ones do. You can test your jokes, you know. Just ask how many of these three jobs they do. If you can't see all three, go back and add the missing ones. It's math, almost.

- *True genius works within form.* Some people bitch against limits. They want to write sitcoms for million-dollar budgets and exotic Arctic locations, but that's not how sitcom works. Sitcom wants to be inexpensive, because it's the relationships and jokes on display, not the spectacle. Don't fight this truth. Embrace it. Demonstrate that you can solve problems creatively and happily within constraints. There's a technical name for people who can do that: working writers.

- *You are not your audience.* While it's great to keep giving them you until you is what they want, keep in mind that your audience is not obsessed with sitcom like you are. They haven't seen every episode of *Blackadder, Dinosaurs* and *Arrested Development* like you have. Remember the difference between the class clown and the class nerd: The class clown tells jokes everyone gets; the class nerd tells jokes only he gets. Be the clown, not the nerd.

- Pacing is important in sitcom. You need to keep things moving. One way to accomplish this is just to keep your characters' speeches short. As a rule of thumb, let no written block of dialogue be longer than it is wide. An exception to this is *the big speech,* which comes at the climax of the episode, where the character has been put under intolerable pressure and, by means of a long and emotional rant, explosively propels himself from denial to acceptance of the theme. See Steve's big speech at the end of the "Inferno" episode of *Coupling* for the classic example.

- The single best way to improve your work is to *let it change.* When I see a writer capable of delivering a second draft that's radically different from her first draft, I know that's a writer committed to serving the work. When I see a writer stuck on a first draft, and stubbornly sticking to the choices she made there, I see defense of ego, and I am not impressed. Change is growth. Embrace change. This is true for sitcom, for all writing, for everything.

- Can your script pass the *random page test?* Any reader should be able to open your script to any page at random and get three things: a laugh or a good solid smile; a sense of what the story is about; a reason to turn the page. If you can't deliver all those goods on every single page, then you still have some work to do. Sometimes it's no fun to demand of yourself that level of excellence, but the best writers do, and if you want to be among their number, then you will, too.

That was eleven, were you keeping count?

Six Quick Things I Know About Writing Jokes

- *Comedy comes from character.* It's vanishingly rare in situation comedy that anyone will tee up a stand-alone joke of the light bulb variety or the knock-knock variety or of any variety at all. Almost every funny thing that happens in sitcom happens because it is filtered through the characters' twisted ways of looking at the world. Don't bother writing jokes. Just have characters do and say and observe things through the funhouse prism of their bent perspective.

- *Quantity breeds quality.* For every ten jokes you try, nine won't work. Don't worry! You only need one (well, one at a time). Don't be afraid to try and try again, and don't be afraid to tell yourself that you can do better. Good news: you *will* do better. As your comic sense becomes refined, you will recognize funny situations faster and exploit their potential more efficiently. Who knows? If you work hard and dare to dream, you might get your success rate up to two in ten.

- *If you must fail, fail big!* When you make jokes for a living, no one expects you to be timid and, really, no one minds very much when you fail. After all, you're trying to do something well that most people can't do at all. So take big chances. Be bold. If you must fail, *fail big*! If nothing else, that shows your willingness and ability to go too far. If you go too far, they can always rein you in, but if you don't learn to push your own envelope, you'll never be better than you are right now.

- *Put the key word last.* A joke is a puzzle, and laughter is the explosive release of tension that comes when the puzzle of the joke is solved. If you put the key word last, then viewers or readers get the information they need in a neat, tight package. If you put the key word elsewhere, they have to move back and forth among the content, collecting information. Tension is diffused and the joke will sputter instead of pop.

- *Sitcom loves sex.* Of course this is not always true. If you're writing the new tween sitcom for Disney, you're unlikely to tell too many dick jokes. But when you're creating your own show, load it up with sexy situations. Make it a rule of your world that sexy situations take place, and that bawdy talk is talked. That way, you'll always have the fertile ground of sex to turn to when you need a quick, cheap laugh. Speaking of cheap laughs...

- *Farts are never not funny.*

That's six, right? Six?

The Five-Minute Promise

Okay, you know what? I think we're pretty much done with this book. There's more I could say, but I intended it to be an overview – something you could dip into and out of as the mood suited you – not a tome. Or maybe I'm just trying to spin laziness into the virtue of brevity. Or saving something for the sequel. It's hard to say. In any case, all this talk about writing sitcoms has got me itching to get back to mine, so I'll wrap things up now with a quick inspirational word, and an offer.

When I'm teaching writers about writing, I always try to provide, "Rules, tools and a good, swift kick in the motivation," and I hope and trust that you've found plenty of all three here. If your motivation flags – which it naturally will from time to time – please remember to take the long view. Today's setbacks or reversals don't matter. Today's rejection letters don't matter. Today's long slogs through bad jokes and leaden scenes don't matter. Better times are coming tomorrow, and fantastically wonderful times lie ahead. I've been walking the writer's road for more than a quarter of a century, and I can tell you that it all gets easier and better and a lot more fun. You gain craft, experience, confidence. Fear falls away. The sheer joy of sitting at the keyboard and making the magic happen eventually comes to replace every other feeling. Let me put it more plainly: It is fucking great to be a writer, and if you don't know that now, you'll find out eventually, so just stick with it.

When you're having trouble sticking with it, do what I do and invoke *the 20-year rule*. The 20-year rule says that if it won't matter in 20 years, it doesn't matter now. And so many things won't matter in 20 years. The gig you thought you had that you lost. The bills you're struggling to pay. The significant other who couldn't hang with your obsession of putting funny words on the page. All that stuff passes away. Everything works out in the end. "Strangely enough, it all turns out well. Why? I don't know. It's a mystery." But it's a wonderful, joyous mystery, this writer's life. It inspires us and gets us high. It makes us feel special and it makes us feel blessed.

And it sure beats working outdoors.

So keep writing. Just keep writing. Everything else will take care of itself. I'm not blowing smoke, just sharing my experience. Where you are, I was. Where I am, you will be. You're living the writer's life. You cannot possibly go wrong.

Finally, there's this: Because we have shared this book together, I now feel like you and I are close personal friends. And though this book may have helped you, as your friend I want to help you even more. So here's my offer. If there comes a time in your writing life when you have a problem you can't solve, I will help you solve it. This could be anything from reframing a joke to solving a story problem or pointing you to a resource or a contact. If this sounds like an incredibly altruistic gesture on my part, well, it is; however, there's a limit to my generosity: I promise to help you any way I can, to the best of my ability, so long as it doesn't take more than five minutes and I don't have to leave my desk.

You'll be amazed at what I can accomplish in five minutes sitting at my desk.

So if writer's block has you in its icy grip, or you don't know how to deal with a nitwit producer, or your mom just told you that your writing sucks and you need someone to hold your hand, I'm here for you, just waiting to receive your email and give you the best five minutes I've got. You can contact me through johnvorhaus.com, and don't feel like you only need to reach out when you have a problem. It'll be great if you just stop in and say hello.

I hope you've enjoyed this book, and I hope you got a lot out of it. Now put it to work. You're going to be amazing. -jV

About the Author

With roots in situation comedy stretching all the way back to *Married... with Children,* JOHN VORHAUS has taught and trained writers worldwide, and created sitcoms of his own in half a dozen countries. He has also written five novels, including the "hippie lit" coming-of-age tale, *Lucy in the Sky.* His classic comedy writing book, *The Comic Toolbox: How to be Funny Even if You're Not,* will be making money for someone long after he's dead, buried and gone. In the meantime, he lives in Southern California, tweets for no apparent reason @TrueFactBarFact and secretly controls the world from www.johnvorhaus.com, where he welcomes your visit.